drinkstuff.com
Barmans Ltd
Saxon Way
Melbourn
Hertfordshire
SG8 6DN
www.drinkstuff.com

ISBN 978-1-5262-0097-6

Published by drinkstuff.com
Printed and bound in China

# Contents

# Introduction

We at drinkstuff felt it was time to give you something to help keep the drinks flowing and the cocktail glasses clinking. Whether you're a cocktail making pro or a beginner with a taste for a Tom Collins, this book is perfect for everyone. We're very proud of our own manufactured cocktail equipment and cocktail making sets, making us all cocktail fanatics, and so, armed with our knowledge, we wrote this book for you!

We'll show you delightful recipes from all the favourite spirits, plus we'll tell you exactly what you'll need in your cocktail kit; from muddler to shaker, this book will become your handy go-to whenever the clock strikes cocktail time. Great for learning the classics, and if you're more experienced, attempting some more daring and creative recipes. We've handpicked each recipe carefully so they're simple to make and tasty to drink.

Not only will you learn how to make a Piña Colada, but we've also been nice enough to show you how to use the two types of cocktail shakers and their tricky quirks, plus we're going to tell about some of the best glasses for your cocktails. Because you wouldn't want to drink a martini from a margarita, now would you?

Be it a bible or a good read, we at drinkstuff present to you 100 Cocktail Recipes.

# Glassware

If you thought there were only a couple of cocktail glasses, you thought wrong. There is a wealth of drinking vessels out there; some specific to cocktails while others are used for numerous drinks. Bartenders and mixologists often like to interpret a drink in their own way, for example, they might serve a champagne cocktail in a martini glass instead of a coupe. Sometimes, it can be hard to keep up with what each glass's purpose is and how to use them correctly. So here's the run-down of the most popular cocktail glasses and what you need to know about them.

1      2      3      4

## 1 Flute

The Flute glass is a stemmed glass with a tall, narrow bowl and was designed to retain the champagne's carbonation. Also, because of its long stem, the drinker can hold the glass without affecting the temperature of the liquid within.

## 2 Piña Colada

The Piña Colada glass, or the 'Poco Grande' has a similar fluted bowl shape to the Hurricane glass but it is shallower and has a longer stem. It is famously used to serve the cocktail Piña Colada.

## 3 Sling

The Sling glass incorporates a lot of different shaped glasses into one; it is tall like the Highball, with a slight inverted bowl like the Martini and it is thin like the Flute. It is commonly used to serve the Singapore Sling cocktail.

## 4 Hurricane

The Hurricane glass got its name from the shape being similar to a hurricane lantern. A tall glass with a fluted bowl shape, typically serves cocktails such as the Hurricane, Blue Hawaii and June Bug.

## 5 Highball
The Highball glass is a tall, slim glass that is often used to serve Long Drinks such as the Tom Collins and the Blood Mary. It is one of the most common cocktail glasses.

## 6 Rocks Tumbler
The Rocks glass, sometimes known as the Old Fashioned or lowball glass is a short tumbler, often used to serve beverages such as whisky. It typically has a wide brim and a thick base.

5      6      7      8

9      10      11      12

## 7 Drinking Jar

The Drinking Jar is a relatively new addition to the glass cabinet. Ten years ago, jars were used to store jam but now they are being used as drinking vessels.

## 8 Copper Cup

The Copper Cup goes hand in hand with the cocktail Moscow Mule and plays a key part in keeping the liquid inside cool and fresh because of the material insulating element.

## 9 Margarita Glass

The Margarita glass is a variant on the classic champagne coupe and are notably used to serve the cocktail, Margarita. However, they are also known to be used for desserts.

## 10 Coupe

Designed especially for sparkling wine and champagne in England in 1663, the champagne coupe or 'champagne saucer' has a shallow, broad bowl and is stemmed.

## 11 Gin Balloon Glass

A large balloon shaped bowl to allow the aromas of the gin to linger, mounted on a long stem to reduce hand warmth from reaching the drink.

## 12 Martini Glass

The Martini glass has a very iconic shape; a long stem with a V shaped bowl, usually with a small volume for serving stronger drinks.

### Hawthorne Strainer (66)
The classic Hawthorne Strainer has a metal spring fixed around the edge of the disc or 'rim' to fit within a mixing glass or shaker tin, and to help strain out the ice as the liquid pours through the several holes on the rim.

### Julep Strainer (5508)
The Julep is a popular strainer for bartenders and mixologists. It's bowl shaped with a handle and fits tightly inside a mixing glass, the liquid then passes through the holes in the bowl while the ice and other solid ingredients stay inside the shaker.

### Fine Mesh Strainer (5520)
A Fine Mesh Strainer features a net or mesh that allows the liquid to pour through but restrains smaller solid ingredients than standard strainers. Often used in conjunction with another standard strainer to achieve a 'double strain'.

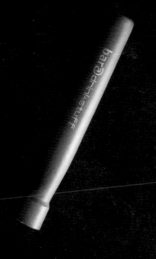

### Muddler (403)
Like a pestle in cooking, a cocktail muddler is used to mash fruits, herbs and spices in the bottom of a shaker tin or glass to release their flavours into the drink. A muddler is an important tool when making classic drinks such as a Mojito or Mint Julep.

### Jigger Measure (6204)
Typically used to measure spirits when making a cocktail, the Jigger Measure has an hourglass figure with unequal sized ends, usually 25ml (single shot) and 50ml (double shot) in the UK.

### Thimble Measures (73)
Giving more variety than a jigger measure, thimble measures come in various sizes including 25ml, 35ml and 50ml to help you measure out cocktail ingredients.

### Bar Spoon (7998)

A Bar Spoon is used for mixing and also layering alcohol in a glass. All bar spoons are long to ensure they can reach the bottom of all types of glasses. A bar spoon can hold approximately 5ml of liquid, equivalent to 1 teaspoon.

### Zester (5467)

A zester is a short handled tool which has a row of round holes with sharpened rims to strip the zest from lemons and other citrus fruit. The tool is pressed and dragged over the skin of the fruit to collect the ribbons through the sharp teeth.

### Reamer (6411)

The reamer is another tool found in the kitchen too and are used to extract the juice from citrus fruits. They have a tapered conical blade with deep straight troughs and there is a smooth spike at the tip.

To purchase these bar tools, search the above codes at www.drinkstuff.com

# Cobbler Shaker

The Cobbler Cocktail shaker is the one that most people start with as it's easier to use than the Boston. It is a three-piece shaker with a built-in strainer and cap, which can be used a measuring cup. It has a unique shape and because of the built-in strainer, it is simpler to use.

## How to Use a Cobbler Shaker

1. Open up the lid and fill with your desired ingredients

2. Place the lid back on firmly, tapping it with the heel of your hand to seal it tight

3. Shake vigorously with your dominant hand for however long is needed

4. Take the cap off of the lid and pour the drink through the built-in strainer

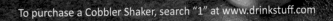

To purchase a Cobbler Shaker, search "1" at www.drinkstuff.com

# Boston Shaker

The Boston Cocktail consists of two pieces made up of a metal can and a glass tumbler. This cocktail shaker, is often favoured by more experienced bartenders and mixologists and is considered more difficult to learn how to use than the all-in-one Cobbler Shaker.

## How to Use a Boston Shaker

1. After filling your mixing glass with your desired ingredients, place the metal half over the glass a slight angle; using the heel of your hand, strike the top twice to ensure a tight seal

2. Shake vigorously, gripping tightly to both halves

3. Holding the bottom half firmly, use the heel of your hand to whack the rim, thus breaking the seal so you're able to separate the two parts

4. With a strainer, hold the shaker in one hand with your forefinger resting on top of the strainer to anchor it in place. Tip the shaker gently and allow the liquid to pour out

To purchase a Boston Shaker, search "1570" at www.drinkstuff.com

# Gin

The spirit, Gin, derives from the flavour of Juniper berries. First evidence of Gin comes from the Middle Ages when it was used medicinally. It became popular when William of Orange, leader of Dutch Republic occupied England and Scotland. It is a broad spirit that varies in style and flavour, but they all have one common factor, which is the juniper. The name Gin comes from 'genievre' which means 'juniper'. Classic cocktails which contain Gin are Martini, Negroni, Gibson and Gin and Tonic.

# Vesper

**Ingredients**
- 50ml of Gin
- 25ml of Vodka
- 10ml of Lillet Blanc
- Lemon Peel, for garnish

**You Will Need**
- Cocktail Shaker
- Strainer

**Method**

Add all of the ingredients to a
Cocktail Shaker filled with ice

Shake until the cocktail shaker is cold
to the touch

Strain into a glass

Garnish with Lemon Peel

## Ingredients

- 50ml of Gin
- 2 tsp of Dry Vermouth
- Ice Cubes
- Lemon Peel, for garnish

## You Will Need

- 50ml Measure
- Mixing Glass
- Bar Spoon
- Strainer

For more information on bar tools, see page 8

# Martini

## Dry Martini | Dirty Martini | Gibson

**Method**

Stir the Gin and Dry Vermouth
in a Mixing Glass filled with ice

Strain into a glass

Garnish with Lemon Peel

- For a Dry Martini, swap the Lemon Peel for Green Olives (avoid oily ones)
- For a Dirty Martini, add a dash of Olive Brine to the Mixing Glass and garnish
with Green Olives
- For a Gibson, swap the Lemon Peel for Cocktail Onions

**Ingredients**
- 50ml of Gin
- 50ml of Sweet Vermouth
- 50ml of Campari
- Ice Cubes
- Orange Slice, for garnish

**You Will Need**
- 50ml Measure
- Cocktail Shaker
- Strainer

For more information on bar tools, see page 8

# Negroni

**Method**

Add all of the ingredients to a Cocktail Shaker filled with ice

Shake until the cocktail shaker is cold to the touch

Strain into an ice filled glass

## Ingredients
- 25ml of Gin
- 70ml of Pineapple Juice
- 3 tsp of Cherry Liqueur
- 2 tsp of Benedictine DOM Liqueur
- 2 tsp of Triple Sec
- 3 tsp of Lime Juice
- 2 tsp of Grenadine
- 1 Dash of Angostura Bitters
- Ice Cubes
- Soda Water
- Cherries, for garnish

## You Will Need
- 25ml Measure
- 70ml Measure
- Cocktail Shaker
- Strainer

# Singapore Sling

## Method

Add all of the ingredients to a
Cocktail Shaker filled with ice

Shake until the cocktail shaker
is cold to the touch

Strain into a glass

Top up with Soda Water

Garnish with Cherries

## Ingredients
- 50ml of Gin
- 25ml of Lemon Juice
- 3 tsp of Simple Syrup
- Soda Water
- Ice Cubes
- Cherries, for garnish
- Orange Slice, for garnish

## You Will Need
- 25ml Measure
- 50ml Measure
- Bar Spoon
- Reamer

For more information on bar tools, see page 8

# Tom Collins

## Method

Add the Gin, Lemon Juice and Simple Syrup to a glass

Stir to combine

Add ice and stir again to chill

Top up with Soda Water and stir again to combine

Garnish with Cherries and an Orange Slice

## Ingredients

- 50ml of Gin
- 25ml of Lime Juice
- 3 tsp of Simple Syrup
- 2 Drops of Angostura Bitters
- Sprig of Mint, for garnish

## You Will Need

- 25ml Measure
- 50ml Measure
- Cocktail Shaker
- Strainer
- Reamer

For more information on bar tools, see page 8

# Southside

**Method**

Add all of the ingredients to a
Cocktail Shaker filled with ice

Shake until the cocktail shaker is
cold to the touch

Strain into a glass

Garnish with a Sprig of Mint

# Gin Fizz

## Ingredients
- 50ml of Gin
- 25ml of Lemon Juice
- 2 Teaspoons of Simple Syrup
- Soda Water
- Ice Cubes
- Lemon Peel, for garnish
- Sprig of Mint, for garnish

## You Will Need
- 25ml Measure
- 50ml Measure
- Cocktail Shaker
- Strainer
- Reamer

## Method

Add the Gin, Lemon Juice and Simple Syrup to a Cocktail Shaker filled with ice

Shake until the cocktail shaker is cold to the touch

Strain into a glass filled with Ice Cubes

Top up with Soda Water

Garnish with a Lemon Peel and a Sprig of Mint

# Gin Rickey

### Ingredients
- 50ml of Gin
- 25ml of Lime Juice
- 2 Teapsoons of Simple Syrup
- Soda Water
- Ice Cubes
- Lime Peel, for garnish

### You Will Need
- 25ml Measure
- 50ml Measure
- Cocktail Shaker
- Strainer
- Reamer

### Method

Add the Gin, Lime Juice and Simple Syrup to a Cocktail Shaker filled with ice

Shake until the cocktail shaker is cold to the touch

Strain into a glass filled with Ice Cubes

Top up with Soda Water

Garnish with a Lime Peel

# Last Word

## Ingredients
- 25ml of Gin
- 25ml of Green Chartreuse Liqueur
- 25ml of Maraschino Liqueur
- 25ml of Lime Juice
- Ice Cubes
- Cherries, for garnish

## You Will Need
- 25ml Measure
- Cocktail Shaker
- Strainer
- Reamer

## Method

Add all the ingredients to a Cocktail Shaker filled with ice

Shake until the cocktail shaker is cold to the touch

Strain into a glass

Garnish with Cherries

# Martinez

**Ingredients**
- 50ml of Gin
- 50ml of Sweet Vermouth
- 1 tsp of Orange Curaçao Liqueur
- 2 Dashes of Angostura Bitters
- Orange Peel, for garnish

**You Will Need**
- 50ml Measure
- MIxing Glass
- Bar Spoon
- Strainer

**Method**

Stir all of the ingredients together in a Mixing Glass filled with ice

Strain into a glass

Garnish with Orange Peel

# White Lady

## Ingredients

- 50ml of Gin
- 25ml of Orange Liqueur
- 25ml of Lemon Juice
- 2 tsp of Simple Syrup
- ½ an Egg White
- Ice Cubes
- Lemon Peel, for garnish

## You Will Need

- 25ml Measure
- 50ml Measure
- Cocktail Shaker
- Strainer
- Reamer

## Method

Add all of the ingredients to a Cocktail Shaker filled with ice

Shake until the cocktail shaker is cold to the touch

Strain back into the same Cocktail Shaker to remove the ice

Shake again without the ice

Pour into a glass

Garnish with Lemon Peel

# Ramos Gin Fizz

## Ingredients

- 50ml of Gin
- 35ml of Single Cream
- 25ml of Simple Syrup
- 1 tsp of Orange flower extract
- 3 tsp of Lemon Juice
- 3 tsp of Lime Juice
- 3 Drops of Vanilla extract
- 1 Egg White
- Ice Cubes
- Soda Water
- Lemon Slice, for garnish
- Sprig of Mint, for garnish

## You Will Need

- 25ml Measure
- 35ml Measure
- 50ml Measure
- Cocktail Shaker
- Strainer
- Reamer

## Method

Add all of the ingredients to a Cocktail Shaker filled with ice

Shake until the cocktail shaker is cold to the touch

Strain into a glass

Top up with Soda Water

Garnish with a Lemon Slice and a Sprig of Mint

# Pink Lady

## Ingredients
- 50ml of Gin
- 25ml of Triple Sec
- 25ml of Lemon Juice
- 2 tsp of Grenadine
- Lemon Peel, for garnish

## You Will Need
- 25ml Measure
- 50ml Measure
- Cocktail Shaker
- Strainer
- Reamer

## Method

Add all of the ingredients to a Cocktail Shaker filled with ice

Shake until the cocktail shaker is cold to the touch

Strain into a glass

Garnish with Lemon Peel

# French 75

## Ingredients
- 50ml of Gin
- 25ml of Lemon Juice
- 2 tsp of Simple Syrup
- Champagne

## You Will Need
- 25ml Measure
- 50ml Measure
- Cocktail Shaker
- Strainer
- Reamer

## Method

Add the Gin, Lemon Juice and Simple Syrup to a Cocktail Shaker filled with ice

Shake until the cocktail shaker is cold to the touch

Strain into a glass

Top up with Champagne

# Bramble

### Ingredients
- 50ml of Gin
- 25ml of Lemon Juice
- 3 tsp of Simple Syrup
- 3 tsp of Blackberry Liqueur
- Crushed Ice
- Lemon Slice and Blackberries for garnish

### You Will Need
- 25ml Measure
- 50ml Measure
- Cocktail Shaker
- Strainer
- Reamer

### Method

Add the Gin, Lemon Juice and Simple Syrup to a Cocktail Shaker filled with ice

Shake until the cocktail shaker is cold to the touch

Strain into a glass filled with Crushed Ice

Pour the Blackberry Liqueur over the drink for bleeding effect

Garnish with a Slice of Lemon and Blackberries

# Salty Dog

## Ingredients
- 50ml of Gin
- 100ml of Grapefruit Juice
- Ice Cubes
- Salt, for garnish
- Slice of Red Grapefruit
  for garnish

## You Will Need
- 50ml Measure
- Cocktail Shaker
- Strainer

## Method

Run a Slice of Red Grapefruit along
the rim of a glass and dip in salt
and fill with ice

Add the Gin and Grapefruit Juice
to a Cocktail Shaker

Shake well until combined

Strain into a glass

# Vodka

Originating from Russia and the surrounding countries, vodka is a distilled drink made up of water and ethanol. It is often made with sugar, fruit and flavourings these days, but traditionally, it is created by the distillation of fermented potatoes and cereal grains. Since 1890, standard Russian vodkas are 40% ABV. It is traditionally drunk neat and sometimes chilled. The earliest evidence of vodka dates back to the 8th century, in Poland. You will see vodka in famous cocktails such as the Cosmopolitan, Black or White Russian, Bloody Mary and Vodka Tonic.

# Harvey Wallbanger

## Ingredients
- 50ml of Vodka
- 3 tsp of Galliano
- Orange Juice
- Ice Cubes
- Orange Slice and Cherries
  for garnish

## You Will Need
- 50ml Measure
- Bar Spoon

## Method

Pour the Vodka and Galliano into
a glass filled with Ice Cubes

Top up with Orange Juice

Stir gently to combine

Garnish with an Orange Slice and
Cherries

**Ingredients**
- 50ml of Vodka
- 3 tsp of Lime Juice
- Ginger Beer
- Lime Wedge, for garnish

**You Will Need**
- 50ml Measure
- Bar Spoon

For more information on bar tools, see page 8

# Moscow Mule

**Method**

Add the Vodka and Lime Juice to a glass, or cup filled with ice

Stir gently to combine

Top up with Ginger Beer

Stir again and garnish with a lime wedge

## Ingredients
- 50ml of Vodka
- 25ml of Coffee Liqueur
- Ice Cubes

## You Will Need
- 25ml Measure
- 50ml Measure
- Bar Spoon

For more information on bar tools, see page 8

# Black Russian
## White Russian

**Method**

Pour the Vodka and Coffee Liqueur into a glass filled with Ice Cubes

Stir gently to combine

For a White Russian, simply add 25ml of Fresh Cream

## Ingredients
- 50ml of Vodka
- 25ml of Blue Curaçao Liqueur
- 100ml of Lemonade
- 25ml of Lime Juice
- 25ml of Simple Syrup
- Ice Cubes
- Orange Slice and Cherries
  for garnish

## You Will Need
– 25ml Measure
- 50ml Measure
- Cocktail Shaker
- Strainer

For more information on bar tools, see page 8.

# Blue Lagoon

### Method

Add the Vodka, Blue Curaçao Liqueur, Lime juice and Simple Syrup into a Cocktail Shaker filled with Ice Cubes

Shake until the Cocktail Shaker is cold to the touch

Strain into a glass filled with Ice Cubes

Top up with Lemonade

Garnish with an Orange Slice and Cherries

**Ingredients**
- 50ml of Vodka
- 25ml of Espresso
- 2 tsp of Coffee Liqueur
- Simple Syrup
- Ice Cubes
- Coffee Beans, for garnish

**You Will Need**
- 25ml Measure
- 50ml Measure
- Cocktail Shaker
- Strainer

For more information on bar tools, see page 8

# Espresso Martini

**Method**

Add all of the ingredients into a
Cocktail Shaker filled with Ice
Cubes

Shake until the Cocktail Shaker is
cold to the touch

Strain into a glass

Garnish with Coffee Beans

## Ingredients

- 50ml of Vodka
- 150ml of Tomato Juice
- 1 tsp of Lemon Juice
- 6 Dashes of Worcestershire Sauce
- 3 Dashes of Tabasco
- Pinch of Salt & Pepper
- Ice Cubes
- Celery Stalk & Lemon Wedge
  for garnish

## You Will Need

- 50ml Measure
- Bar Spoon

For more information on bar tools, see page 8

# Bloody Mary

### Method

Add Vodka and Tomato Juice
to a glass filled with Ice Cubes

Add the Worcestershire
Sauce, Tabasco, Lemon Juice,
Salt & Pepper to the glass

Stir gently to combine

Garnish with a Celery Stalk
and Lemon Wedge

## Ingredients
- 25ml of Vodka
- 25ml of Orange Liqueur
- 50ml of Cranberry Juice
- 3 tsp of Lime Juice
- Ice Cubes
- Lemon Slice, for garnish

## You Will Need
- 25ml Measure
- 50ml Measure
- Cocktail Shaker
- Strainer

For more information on bar tools, see page 8

# Cosmopolitan
## Champagne Cosmopolitan

**Method**

Add the Vodka, Orange Liqueur, and Fruit Juices to a Cocktail Shaker filled with Ice Cubes

Shake until the Cocktail Shaker is cold to the touch

Strain into a glass

Garnish with a Lemon Slice

For a Champagne Cosmopolitan, simply add 50ml of Champagne

## Ingredients

- 25ml of Vodka
- 25ml of White Rum
- 25ml of Gin
- 25ml of Triple Sec
- 25ml of Tequila
- 25ml of Simple Syrup
- 35ml of Lemon Juice
- Cola
- Lemon Twist, for garnish

## You Will Need

- 25ml Measure
- 35ml Measure
- Bar Spoon

For more information on bar tools, see page 8

# Long Island Iced Tea

**Method**

Add all of the ingredients to an ice filled glass

Stir gently to combine

Top up with cola

Stir again

Garnish with a Lemon Twist

# Mudslide

**Ingredients**
- 50ml of Vodka
- 50ml of Irish Cream
- 50ml of Coffee Liqueur
- 3 Scoops of Vanilla Ice Cream
- Chocolate Syrup, for garnish

**You Will Need**
- 50ml Measure
- Mixing glass
- Bar Spoon

**Method**

Add all of the ingredients to a Mixing Glass

Mix until smooth

Pour the mixture into a glass and drizzle with Chocolate Syrup

# Screaming Orgasm

## Ingredients

- 35ml of Vodka
- 35ml of Coffee Liqueur
- 35ml of Amaretto
- 35ml of Irish Cream
- 35ml of Single Cream
- 35ml of Milk
- Ice Cubes

## You Will Need

- 35ml Measure
- Cocktail Shaker
- Strainer

## Method

Add all of the ingredients to a Cocktail Shaker filled with Ice Cubes

Shake until the Cocktail Shaker is cold to the touch

Strain into an ice filled glass

# Sex on the Beach

### Ingredients
- 50ml of Vodka
- 25ml of Peach Schnapps
- 50ml of Orange Juice
- 50ml of Cranberry Juice
- Orange Slice, for garnish

### You Will Need
- 25ml Measure
- 50ml Measure
- Bar Spoon

### Method

Add all of the ingredients to an ice filled glass

Stir gently to combine

Garnish with an Orange Slice

# Woo Woo

## Ingredients
- 50ml of Vodka
- 25ml of Peach Schnapps
- 75ml of Cranberry Juice
- Lime Wedge, for garnish

## You Will Need
- 25ml Measure
- 50ml Measure
- Bar Spoon

## Method

Add all of the ingredients to an ice filled glass

Stir gently to combine

Garnish with a Lime Wedge

**Ingredients**
- 50ml of Vodka
- 25ml of Raspberry Liqueur
- 50ml of Pineapple Juice
- Ice Cubes
- Raspberries and Lemon Peel
  for garnish

**You Will Need**
- 25ml Measure
- 50ml Measure
- Cocktail Shaker
- Strainer

For more information on bar tools, see page 8.

# French Martini

## Method

Add all of the ingredients into a
Cocktail Shaker filled with Ice
Cubes

Shake until the Cocktail Shaker is
cold to the touch

Strain into a glass

Garnish with Raspberries and
Lemon Peel

# Appletini

## Ingredients
- 50ml of Vodka
- 25ml of Apple Schnapps
- 2 tsp of Vermouth
- Ice Cubes
- Apple Slice & Cherries, for garnish

## You Will Need
- 25ml Measure
- 50ml Measure
- Cocktail Shaker
- Strainer

## Method

Add all of the ingredients into a Cocktail Shaker filled with Ice Cubes

Shake until the Cocktail Shaker is cold to the touch

Strain into a glass

Garnish with an Apple Slice and Cherries

# Porn Star Martini

### Ingredients
- 50ml of Vanilla Vodka
- 25ml of Passion Fruit Liqueur
- 2 tsp of Passion Fruit Puree
- 50ml of Champagne
- Ice Cubes
- Passion Fruit, for garnish

### You Will Need
- 25ml Measure
- 50ml Measure
- Cocktail Shaker
- Strainer

### Method

Add all of the ingredients excluding the Champagne into a Cocktail Shaker filled with Ice Cubes

Shake until the Cocktail Shaker is cold to the touch

Strain into a glass

Add champagne to a shot glass and serve as a chaser between sips

Garnish with half a Passion Fruit

# Californication

## Ingredients
- 25ml of Vodka
- 25ml of Gin
- 25ml of White Rum
- 25ml of Tequila
- 3 tsp of Orange Liqueur
- 3 tsp of Lemon Juice
- Ice Cubes
- Orange Juice
- Orange Slice, for garnish

## You Will Need
- 25ml Measure
- Bar Spoon

## Method

Add the Vodka, Gin, White Rum, Tequila, Orange Liqueur and Lemon Juice to a glass filled with Ice Cubes

Stir gently to combine

Top up with the Orange Juice

Garnish with an Orange Slice

# Absolutely Fabulous

**Ingredients**
- 25ml of Vodka
- 25ml of Cranberry Juice
- Prosecco
- Ice Cubes
- Raspberries, for garnish

**You Will Need**
- 25ml Measure
- Cocktail Shaker
- Strainer

**Method**

Add Vodka and Cranberry Juice to a Cocktail Shaker filled with Ice Cubes

Shake until the Cocktail Shaker is cold to the touch

Strain into a glass

Top up with Prosecco

Garnish with Raspberries

# Seabreeze

**Ingredients**
- 35ml of Vodka
- 125ml of Cranberry Juice
- 25ml of Grapefruit Juice
- Lime Wedge, for garnish

**You Will Need**
- 25ml Measure
- 35ml Measure
- Cocktail Shaker
- Strainer

**Method**

Add all of the ingredients to a Cocktail Shaker filled with Ice Cubes

Shake until the Cocktail Shaker is cold to the touch

Strain into an ice filled glass

Garnish with a Lime Wedge

# Key West Cooler

## Ingredients
- 25ml of Vodka
- 25ml of Melon Liqueur
- 25ml of Peach Schnapps
- 25ml of Coconut Rum
- 75ml of Cranberry Juice
- 75ml of Orange Juice
- Orange Slice, for garnish

## You Will Need
- 25ml Measure
- Cocktail Shaker
- Strainer

## Method

Fill a glass with Crushed Ice and pour in the Melon Liqueur

Add the Peach Schnapps, Coconut Rum and Orange Juice to a Cocktail Shaker filled with Ice Cubes

Shake until the Cocktail Shaker is cold to the touch

Strain into the glass, creating a second layer

Add the Vodka and Cranberry Juice to a Cocktail Shaker filled with Ice Cubes, shake and strain into the glass, creating a third, and final layer

Garnish with an Orange Slice

# Root Beer Float

**Ingredients**
- 50ml of Vodka
- 1 Can of Root Beer
- 4 Scoops of Vanilla Ice Cream
- Whipped Cream

**You Will Need**
- 50ml Measure

**Method**

Scoop the Vanilla Ice Cream into a glass

Add the Vodka and Root Beer

Garnish with Whipped Cream

# Kamikaze

## Ingredients
- 50ml of Vodka
- 25ml of Orange Liqueur
- 25ml of Lime Juice
- Lime Slice, for garnish

## You Will Need
- 25ml Measure
- 50ml Measure
- Cocktail Shaker
- Strainer
- Reamer

## Method

Add all of the ingredients to a Cocktail Shaker filled with ice

Shake until the cocktail shaker is cold to the touch

Strain into a glass

Garnish with a Lime Slice

# Rum

Made from sugarcane byproducts (molasses) or sugarcane juice and created using a fermentation and distillation process, rum is usually aged in barrels and is produced the most in the Caribbean and Latin America. There is much debate as to when and where rum originates from, but some believe fermented drinks produced from sugarcane were first made in ancient India or China. Like its origin, rum's name is often debated too. Is it cockney rhyming slang for 'the best' or is it the Romani word 'rum' meaning 'strong' or 'potent'? Drunk famously by the navy and often nicknamed 'grog' when mixed with water, rum is commonly drunk neat as well as in mixers such as the Daiquiri, Mojito, Hurricane, Long Island Iced Tea and Piña Colada.

# Bahama Mama

### Ingredients
- 25ml of Dark Rum
- 25ml of Aged Spiced Rum
- 35ml of Coconut Rum
- 50ml of Orange Juice
- 75ml of Pineapple Juice
- 3 Dashes of Angostura Bitters
- Pineapple Wedge & Cherry
  for garnish

### You Will Need
- 25ml Measure
- 35ml Measure
- 50ml Measure
- Cocktail Shaker
- Strainer

### Method

Measure out the 3 different rums
into a cocktail shaker

Measure out the 2 fruit juices and
add to the cocktail shaker

Add 3 dashes of Angostura Bitters

Top up the cocktail shaker with ice

Shake until the cocktail shaker is
cold to the touch

Strain into an ice filled glass

Garnish with a pineapple wedge
and cherry

## Ingredients

- 50ml of White Rum
- 25ml of Blue Curaçao Liqueur
- 50ml of Coconut Cream
- 100ml of Pineapple Juice
- Dash of Lemon Juice
- Crushed ice
- Pineapple Wedge & Cherry
  for garnish

## You Will Need

- 25ml Measure
- 50ml Measure
- Cocktail Shaker
- Strainer
- Bar Knife

For more information on bar tools, see page 8

# Blue Hawaiian

## Method

Measure out the white rum and blue curaçao into a cocktail shaker

Measure out the pineapple juice and coconut cream and add to the cocktail shaker

Add a dash of lemon juice

Shake until the cocktail shaker is cold to the touch

Pour the cocktail into a glass

Garnish with a pineapple wedge and cherry

# Banana Daiquiri

## Ingredients
- 50ml of White Rum
- 25ml of Lime Juice
- 50ml of Banana Flavoured Liqueur
- 1 Banana
- Crushed Ice

## You Will Need
- 25ml Measure
- 50ml Measure
- Blender

## Method

Add all of the ingredients to a blender with crushed ice

Blend until smooth and combined

Pour the cocktail into a glass

# Strawberry Daiquiri

### Ingredients
- 50ml of White Rum
- 25ml of Lime Juice
- 1 Teaspoon of Simple Syrup
- 5 Large Strawberries
- Crushed Ice

### You Will Need
- 25ml Measure
- 50ml Measure
- Blender

### Method

Add all of the ingredients to a blender

Blend until smooth and combined

Pour the cocktail over crushed ice into a glass

**Ingredients**
- 50ml of White Rum
- 35ml of Fresh Lime Juice
- 4 tsp of Simple Syrup
- Lime Wedge, for garnish

**You Will Need**
- 35ml Measure
- 50ml Measure
- Cocktail Shaker
- Strainer
- Bar Knife
- Reamer

For more information on bar tools, see page 8

# Daiquiri
## Hemingway Daiquiri

**Method**

Add all of the ingredients to an ice filled cocktail shaker

Shake until the cocktail shaker is cold to the touch

Strain into a glass

Garnish with a wedge of a lime

To change a Daiquiri into a Hemingway Daiquiri simply add 10ml of
Cherry Liqueur and 25ml of Grapefruit Juice

## Ingredients
- 50ml of Cachaça
  (also known as Brazilian rum)
- 3 tsp of Sugar
- 1 Lime
- Ice Cubes

## You Will Need
- 50ml Measure
- Bar knife
- Muddler
- Bar Spoon

For more information on bar tools, see page 8

# Caipirinha

**Method**

Quarter the Lime and add to the glass along with the Sugar

Use the muddler to combine the Lime and the Sugar together

Fill the glass with Ice Cubes

Add the Cachaça and stir

## Ingredients
- 50ml of White Rum
- 35ml of Dark Rum
- 35ml of Orange Juice
- 35ml of Pineapple Juice
- 3 tsp of Lime Juice
- 2 tsp of Passion Fruit Syrup
- 2 tsp of Grenadine
- Crushed Ice
- Orange Slice and Cherry

## You Will Need
- 35ml Measure
- 50ml Measure
- Cocktail Shaker
- Strainer
- Bar Knife

For more information on bar tools, see page 8

# Hurricane

## Method

Measure out the Rums and add to a cocktail shaker filled with ice

Add the Fruit Juices, Passion Fruit Syrup and Grenadine to the cocktail shaker

Shake until the cocktail shaker is cold to the touch

Strain into a glass filled with Crushed Ice

Garnish with a slice of Orange and a Cherry

## Ingredients

- 35ml of Spiced Rum
- 25ml of Coconut Flavoured Rum
- 100ml of Pineapple Juice
- 50ml of Orange Juice
- 1 tsp of Grenadine
- Ice Cubes

## You Will Need

- 25ml Measure
- 35ml Measure
- 50ml Measure
- Cocktail Shaker
- Strainer

For more information on bar tools, see page 8

# Mai Tai

## Method

Add all of the ingredients to a cocktail shaker with ice

Shake until the cocktail shaker is cold to the touch

Strain into a glass filled with Ice Cubes

## Ingredients

- 50ml of White Rum
- 1 Lime
- Handful of Mint Leaves
- Soda Water
- Crushed Ice

## You Will Need

- 50ml Measure
- Muddler
- Bar Knife

# Mojito

**Method**

Quarter the Lime and squeeze the juice into a glass

Add the Mint Leaves and muddle the Mint and Lime Juice together

Fill the glass with Crushed Ice

Pour the rum over the ice

Top up with Soda Water

Garnish with a Mint Sprig and add a straw

## Ingredients
- 50ml of Coconut Rum
- 25ml of Coconut Cream
- 75ml of Pineapple Juice
- Crushed Ice
- Fresh Pineapple Wedges
  for garnish

## You Will Need
- 25ml Measure
- 50ml Measure
- Blender

For more information on bar tools, see page 8

# Piña Colada

## Method

Add the Coconut Rum, Coconut Cream, Pineapple Juice and Crushed Ice to a blender

Blend until smooth

Pour into a glass and garnish with pineapple wedges

## Ingredients

- 25ml of White Rum
- 25ml of Dark Rum
- 25ml of Golden Rum
- 25ml of Apricot Brandy
- 25ml of Orange Cognac Liqueur
- 75ml of Orange Juice
- 75ml of Pineapple Juice
- 35ml of Lime Juice
- 3 tsp of Grenadine
- Crushed ice

## You Will Need

- 25ml Measure
- 35ml Measure
- Cocktail Shaker
- Strainer

For more information on bar tools, see page 8

# Zombie

## Method

Add all of the ingredients to a
Cocktail Shaker filled with ice

Shake until the cocktail shaker is
cold to the touch

Strain into a glass filled with
Crushed Ice

Garnish with your choice of exotic
fruit

## Ingredients

- 50ml of Dark Rum
- 25ml of Vermouth
- 75ml of Pressed Apple Juice
- 3 tsp of Lime Juice
- 2 tsp of Simple Syrup
- Ice Cubes
- Cinnamon Stick, for garnish

## You Will Need

- 25ml Measure
- 50ml Measure
- Cocktail Shaker
- Strainer

For more information on bar tools, see page 8.

# Voodoo

**Method**

Add all of the ingredients to a Cocktail Shaker filled with ice

Shake until the cocktail shaker is cold to the touch

Strain into a glass filled with Ice Cubes

Garnish with the Cinnamon Stick

## Ingredients

- 50ml of Spiced Rum
- 2 tsp of Honey
- 1 Knob of Unsalted Butter
- Warm Apple Cider
- Freshly Grated Nutmeg, a Cinnamon Stick, and Orange Peel for garnish

## You Will Need

- 50ml Measure
- Bar Spoon

For more information on bar tools, see page 8

# Hot Buttered Rum

## Method

Add the Butter and Honey to a glass or mug

Add the Warm Apple Cider to melt the Butter and Honey

Add the Spiced Rum and stir to combine

Sprinkle the grated nutmeg into the glass

Use the Cinnamon Stick and Orange Peel to garnish

## Ingredients

- 50ml of White Rum
- 50ml of Vermouth
- 1 tsp of Orange Curaçao
- ½ a tsp of Grenadine
- Orange Peel, for garnish

## You Will Need

- 50ml Measure
- Cocktail Shaker
- Strainer

For more information on bar tools, see page 8

# El Presidente

**Method**

Add all of the ingredients to a Cocktail Shaker filled with ice

Shake until the cocktail shaker is cold to the touch

Strain into a glass

Garnish with Orange Peel

# Painkiller

## Ingredients
- 50ml of Dark Rum
- 50ml of Pineapple Juice
- 50ml of Orange Juice
- 25ml of Coconut Cream
- Pineapple Wedge and Cherry
  for garnish
- Freshly Grated Nutmeg
- Ice Cubes

## You Will Need
- 25ml Measure
- 50ml Measure
- Cocktail Shaker
- Bar Spoon

## Method

Add the Rum, Fruit Juices
and Coconut Cream to a
Cocktail Shaker

Lightly shake to combine
the ingredients

Add Ice Cubes to a glass

Pour the cocktail into the
glass

Garnish with pineapple wedge, cherry and sprinkle
the nutmeg on top

# Dark and Stormy

**Ingredients**
- 50ml of Dark Rum
- Ginger Beer
- Wedge of Lime

**You Will Need**
- 50ml Measure
- Bar Knife

**Method**

Pour the Ginger Beer to an ice filled glass

Add the Dark Rum to create a bleeding effect

Squeeze the lime into the cocktail and place for garnish

# Rum Punch

## Ingredients
**To make approximately 2 litres**
- 500ml of Dark Rum
- 250ml of White Rum
- 500ml of Pineapple Juice
- 500ml of Orange Juice
- 35ml of Grenadine Syrup
- 8 Limes
- 8 Drops of Angostura Bitters
- Grated Nutmeg
- Soda Water (optional)
- Crushed Ice
- Pineapple slices, for garnish

## You Will Need
- 25ml Measure
- 35ml Measure
- 50ml Measure
- Punch Bowl
- Reamer
- Bar Knife
- Bar Spoon

## Method

Use a Reamer to extract the juice from the Limes

Add the Lime Juice to a Punch Bowl along with the other ingredients

Refrigerate for at least 1 hour

Stir gently to mix together

Garnish with Pineapple Slices and add Crushed Ice

# Planter's Punch

## Ingredients
- 50ml of Dark Rum
- 2 tsp of Grenadine
- 50ml of Pineapple Juice
- 50ml of Orange Juice
- 50ml of Passionfruit Juice
- Soda Water (optional)
- Seasonal Fruit, to garnish
- Ice Cubes

## You Will Need
- 50ml Measure
- Cocktail Shaker
- Strainer

## Method

Add the Rum, Fruit Juices and Grenadine to a Cocktail Shaker filled with ice

Shake until the cocktail shaker is cold to the touch

Strain into a glass filled with Ice Cubes

Top up with Soda Water (optional)

Garnish with seasonal fruits

# Eggnog

## Ingredients

- 35ml of Dark Rum
- 125ml of Whole Milk
- 50ml of Double Cream
- ¼ Vanilla Pod, split and seeded
- 1 Egg
- 5 tsp of Granulated Sugar
- Grated Nutmeg, for garnish
- Cinnamon Stick, for garnish

## You Will Need

- 25ml Measure
- 35ml Measure
- 50ml Measure
- Cocktail Shaker
- Strainer

## Method

Add all of the ingredients to a
Cocktail Shaker

Shake until the cocktail shaker is
cold to the touch

Pour into a glass

Garnish with Grated Nutmeg and a
Cinnamon Stick

# June Bug

## Ingredients

- 25ml of Coconut Flavoured Rum
- 25ml of Melon Liqueur
- 25ml of Banana Liqueur
- 125ml of Pineapple Juice
- 25ml of Lime Juice
- Ice Cubes
- Pineapple Wedge, for garnish

## You Will Need

- 25ml Measure
- 50ml Measure
- Cocktail Shaker
- Strainer
- Reamer

## Method

Add the Rums, Liqueurs and Fruit Juices to a Cocktail Shaker filled with ice

Shake until the cocktail shaker is cold to the touch

Strain into a glass filled with Ice Cubes

Garnish with a Pineapple Wedge

# Tequila

First produced in the 16th century near the city of Tequila, Mexico, the distilled beverage is made from the blue agave plant which grows in the highlands of the state Jalisco. Mexican law states that tequila can only made in the state of Jalisco and a limited few other states and is often made at 33-40% ABV. Tequila is bottled in five different categories depending on how long they've been aged and what they've been flavoured with. Often served in shot glasses and paired with salt and lime, there are also a lot of cocktails that contain tequila; the Margarita, Tequila Sunrise and Paloma to name a few. Plus good quality tequila is drunk neat.

# La Paloma

**Ingredients**
- 70ml of Tequila
- 70ml of Pink Grapefruit Juice
- 25ml of Lime Juice
- Grapefruit Soda
- Ice Cubes
- Salt, for the rim
- Lime Wedge, for garnish

**You Will Need**
- 25ml Measure
- 70ml Measure
- Cocktail Shaker
- Reamer

**Method**

Run a Wedge of Lime along the rim of a glass and dip in salt

Add Ice Cubes, Tequila and the Fruit Juices to a Cocktail Shaker

Shake until the cocktail shaker is cold to the touch

Pour into the glass

Top up with Grapefruit Soda

Garnish with a Lime Wedge

## Ingredients
- 50ml of Tequila
- 25ml of Lime Juice
- 2 tsp of Simple Syrup
- Ginger Beer
- Ice Cubes
- Lime Wedge, for garnish

## You Will Need
- 25ml Measure
- 50ml Measure
- Cocktail Shaker
- Strainer
- Bar Spoon

For more information on bar tools, see page 8

# Mexican Mule

**Method**

Add the Tequila, Lime Juice and Simple Syrup to a Cocktail Shaker filled with Ice Cubes

Shake until the cocktail shaker is cold to the touch

Strain into an ice filled glass

Top up with Ginger Beer

Stir gently to combine

## Ingredients

- 50ml of Tequila
- 25ml of Orange Liqueur
- 25ml of Lime Juice
- 1 Teaspoon of Agave Syrup
- Ice Cubes
- Salt, for the rim
- Lime Wedge, for the garnish

## You Will Need

- 25ml Measure
- 50ml Measure
- Cocktail Shaker
- Strainer

For more information on bar tools, see page 8

# Margarita

**Method**

Run a Wedge of Lime along the rim of a glass and dip in salt

Add all the ingredients to a Cocktail Shaker filled with Ice Cubes

Shake until the cocktail shaker is cold to the touch

Strain into the glass

Garnish with a Lime Wedge

## Ingredients
- 50ml of Tequila
- 100ml of Orange Juice
- 3 tsp of Grenadine
- Ice Cubes
- Orange Slice and Cherries, for garnish

## You Will Need
- 50ml Measure
- Cocktail Shaker
- Strainer

For more information on bar tools, see page 8

# Tequila Sunrise

## Method

Place 3 tsp of Grenadine into a glass and fill with Ice Cubes

Add the Tequila and Orange Juice to a Cocktail Shaker filled with Ice Cubes

Shake until the cocktail shaker is cold to the touch

Strain into the glass

Garnish with an Orange Slice and Cherries

## Ingredients
- 50ml of Tequila
- 50ml of Soda Water
- 35ml of Lemon & Lime Soda
- 1 Lime
- 3 tsp of Sugar
- Crushed Ice
- Handful of Mint Leaves
- Lime Slice, for garnish

## You Will Need
- 35ml Measure
- 50ml Measure
- Muddler
- Bar Knife

For more information on bar tools, see page 8

# Mexican Mojito

## Method

Quarter the Lime and squeeze
the juice into a glass

Add the Mint Leaves and Sugar to
the glass and muddle together

Fill the glass with Crushed Ice

Pour the Tequila over the ice

Top up with Soda Water and
Lemon & Lime Soda

Garnish with a Mint Sprig

# El Diablo

## Ingredients
- 50ml of Tequila
- 50ml of Blackcurrant Liqueur
- 50ml of Lime Juice
- Ginger Beer
- Ice Cubes
- Lime Wedge, for garnish

## You Will Need
- 50ml Measure
- Bar Spoon

## Method

Fill a glass with Ice Cubes

Add the Tequila, Blackcurrant
Liqueur and Lime Juice

Stir gently to combine

Top up with Ginger Beer

Garnish with a Lime Wedge

# Silk Stocking

**Ingredients**
- 50ml of White Tequila
- 25ml of White Chocolate Liqueur
- 25ml of Single Cream
- Ice Cubes
- 2 tsp of Grenadine
- Raspberries, for garnish

**You Will Need**
- 25ml Measure
- 50ml Measure
- Cocktail Shaker
- Strainer

**Method**

Add all of the ingredients to a Cocktail Shaker filled with Ice Cubes

Shake until the cocktail shaker is cold to the touch

Strain into a glass

Garnish with Raspberries

# Whisky

Whisky or 'whiskey' is made from fermenting grain mash; grains such as barley, corn, rye and wheat. It is almost always aged in wooden casks and the time of aging varies from whisky to whisky (to whiskey). Though there are a lot of different types of whiskies out there, they all have three things in common; the fermentation of grains process, the distillation and the aging in wooden casks. When spelt 'whiskey', it is usually referring to American or Irish produced whiskey, while 'whisky' is used when describing Scottish and other countries' whisky. Earliest evidence of distillation is from ancient Mesopotamia (2nd Millennium BC). The practice spread across Europe and to Scotland and Ireland in the 15th century where it was used to create medicine. First written record of whisky comes from Ireland, circa 1400. Whisky is commonly drunk neat or with ice, but it can be seen in some cocktails too; Manhattan and Sazerac being just two.

# Whiskey Sour

**Ingredients**
- 50ml of Bourbon Whisky
- 50ml of Lemon Juice
- 25ml of Simple Syrup
- Cherries, for garnish

**You Will Need**
- 25ml Measure
- 50ml Measure
- Cocktail Shaker
- Strainer
- Reamer

**Method**

Add all of the ingredients to a Cocktail Shaker filled with ice

Shake until the Cocktail Shaker is cold to the touch

Strain into an ice filled glass

Garnish with Cherries

## Ingredients

- 75ml of Whisky
- 35ml of Sweet Vermouth
- 3 Dashes of Angostura Bitters
- Orange Peel, for garnish

## You Will Need

- 25ml Measure
- 35ml Measure
- Mixing Glass
- Bar Spoon
- Strainer

For more information on bar tools, see page 8

# Manhattan

**Method**

Add the ingredients into a Mixing Glass filled with ice

Stir gently to combine

Strain into a glass

Garnish with Orange Peel

## Ingredients

- 50ml of Whisky
- 1 Sugar Cube
- 3 Dashes of Angostura Bitters
- Soda Water
- Ice Cube

## You Will Need

- 50ml Measure
- Muddler
- Bar Spoon

For more information on bar tools, see page 8

# Old Fashioned

**Method**

Place the Sugar Cube in a glass

Add the bitters and a dash of Soda water to saturate the sugar cube

Muddle the ingredients together until they dissolve

Add an ice cube to the glass

Add the Whisky and stir gently to combine

## Ingredients
- 75ml of Bourbon
- 25ml of Simple Syrup
- Handful of Mint Leaves
- Crushed Ice

## You Will Need
- 25ml Measure
- Muddler
- Bar Spoon

For more information on bar tools, see page 8

# Mint Julep

**Method**

Add the Simple Syrup and Mint into a glass and muddle together

Add the Bourbon to the glass

Pack the glass halfway with Crushed Ice

Stir gently to combine and the glass is frosted on the outside

Top the glass up with more Crushed Ice creating an ice dome

Garnish with a Sprig of Mint

## Ingredients
- 50ml of Scotch
- 25ml of Single Malt Scotch
- 25ml of Lemon juice
- 3 tsp of Ginger Syrup
- 3 tsp of Honey
- Ice Cubes
- Candied Ginger, for garnish

## You Will Need
- 25ml Measure
- 50ml Measure
- Cocktail Shaker
- Strainer

For more information on bar tools, see page 8.

# Penicillin

**Method**

Add all of the ingredients to a Cocktail Shaker filled with ice

Shake until the Cocktail Shaker is cold to the touch

Strain into an ice filled glass

Garnish with Candied Ginger

# Brooklyn

## Ingredients
- 50ml of Whisky
- 50ml of Vermouth
- 2 tsp of Orange Liqueur
- 2 tsp of Cherry Liqueur
- Ice Cubes
- Cherries, for garnish

## You Will Need
- 50ml Measure
- Mixing Glass
- Strainer
- Bar Spoon

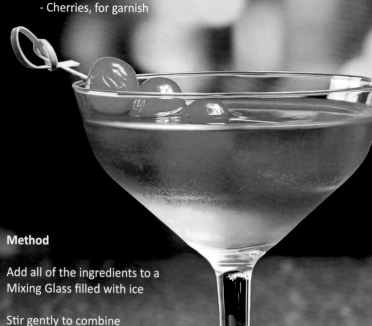

## Method

Add all of the ingredients to a
Mixing Glass filled with ice

Stir gently to combine

Strain into a glass

Garnish with Cherries

# Rob Roy

## Ingredients

- 50ml of Scotch
- 25ml of Vermouth
- 2 Dashes of Angostura Bitters
- 1 tsp Maraschino Cherry Syrup
- Lemon Peel, for garnish

## You Will Need

- 25ml Measure
- 50ml Measure
- MIxing Glass
- Bar Spoon
- Strainer

## Method

Add the ingredients to a MIxing
Glass filled with ice

Stir gently to combine

Strain into a glass

Garnish with Lemon Peel

# Hot Toddy

## Ingredients
- 50ml of Whisky
- 25ml of Lemon Juice
- 25ml of Simple Syrup
- 1 Teaspoon of Honey
- Boiling Water
- Lemon Slice and Cinnamon
  Stick, for garnish

## You Will Need
- 25ml Measure
- 50ml Measure
- Bar Spoon
- Reamer

## Method

Drizzle the Honey into a glass

Add the Whisky, Lemon Juice
and Simple Syrup

Stir gently to combine

Top up the glass with Boiling
Water

Stir again to combine

Garnish with a Lemon Slice
and Cinnamon Stick

# Irish Coffee

## Ingredients
- 50ml of Whisky
- 200ml Black Coffee
- 3 tsp of Simple Syrup
- Whipped Cream

## You Will Need
- 50ml Measure
- Bar Spoon

## Method

Add the Freshly Brewed Coffee to a heat resistant glass

Add the Simple Syrup and stir

Pour in the Whisky and stir to combine

Add Whipped Cream as desired

# Horse's Neck

### Ingredients
- 50ml of Bourbon
- 3 Dashes of Angostura Bitters
- Ginger Ale
- Ice Cubes
- Lemon Peel, for garnish

### You Will Need
- 50ml Measure
- Bar Spoon

### Method

Add ice to a glass

Add the Bourbon and Bitters

Stir to combine

Top up with Ginger Ale

Garnish with Lemon Peel

# Rattlesnake

## Ingredients
- 50ml of Bourbon
- 2 tsp of Lemon Juice
- 2 tsp of Sugar Syrup
- 1 Teaspoon of Absinthe
- ½ an Egg White
- Ice Cubes

## You Will Need
- 50ml Measure
- Cocktail Shaker
- Strainer

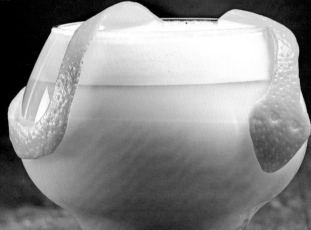

## Method

Add all of the ingredients to a Cocktail Shaker filled with ice

Shake until the cocktail shaker is cold to the touch

Strain into a glass

# Vieux Carré

## Ingredients
- 25ml of Whisky
- 25ml of Cognac
- 25ml of Sweet Vermouth
- 1 Teaspoon of Galliano Liqueur
- 2 Dashes of Peychaud's Bitters
- 2 Dashes of Angostura Bitters

## You Will Need
- 25ml Measure
- Mixing Glass
- Bar Spoon

## Method

Add the ingredients to a MIxing Glass filled with ice

Stir gently to combine

Pour into a glass

# Bee Sting

**Ingredients**
- 25ml of Whisky
- 25ml of Tequila
- 50ml of Apple Juice
- 1 tsp Honey
- Ginger Ale
- Ice Cubes
- Lemon Slice, for garnish

**You Will Need**
- 25ml Measure
- 50ml Measure
- Cocktail Shaker
- Strainer

**Method**

Drizzle the Honey in to a
Cocktail Shaker filled with ice

Add the Whisky, Tequila and
Apple Juice

Shake until the cocktail
shaker is cold to the touch

Strain into an ice filled glass

Top up with Ginger Ale

Garnish with a Lemon Slice

# Rusty Nail

### Ingredients
- 50ml of Scotch Whisky
- 25ml of Drambuie
- Lemon Peel, for garnish

### You Will Need
- 25ml Measure
- 50ml Measure
- Mixing Glass
- Bar Spoon

## Method

Add the ingredients to a MIxing Glass filled with ice

Stir gently to combine

Pour into a glass

Garnish with Lemon Peel

# Alabama Slammer

## Ingredients
- 25ml of Bourbon
- 25ml of Sloe Gin
- 25ml of Almond Liqueur
- 50ml of Orange Juice
- Orange Slice and Cherries
  for garnish

## You Will Need
- 25ml Measure
- 50ml Measure
- Bar Spoon

## Method

Add the Bourbon, Sloe Gin and
Almond Liqueur to an ice filled
glass

Top up with Orange Juice

Stir gently to combine

Garnish with an Orange Slice and
Cherries

# Amaretto Sour

## Ingredients
- 50ml of Almond Liqueur
- 25ml of Bourbon
- 25ml of Lemon Juice
- 1 tsp of Simple Syrup
- ½ an Egg White
- Ice Cubes
- Orange Slice and Cherries
  for garnish

## You Will Need
- 25ml Measure
- 50ml Measure
- Cocktail Shaker
- Strainer

## Method

Add all of the ingredients to a
Cocktail Shaker filled with ice

Shake until the cocktail shaker is
cold to the touch

Strain into a glass

Garnish with an Orange Slice and
Cherries

# Godfather

### Ingredients
- 50ml of Scotch
- 25ml of Almond Liqueur

### You Will Need
- 25ml Measure
- 50ml Measure
- Bar Spoon

### Method

Add the ingredients into a glass filled with ice

Stir gently to combine

# Wine, Champagne and Brandy

Made from fermented grapes and sometimes other fruits, wine gets its name from the Latin word 'vinum'. Grapes ferment without the addition of sugars or acids and has been produced for thousands of years. Much celebrated by the Greeks, Romans and Egyptians, there are three common types of wine; red, white and rose, with the wine family extending to sparkling wine (like Champagne or Prosecco), spirits distilled from wine, such as Brandy, and fortified wines like Port and Sherry. There are plenty of cocktails containing wine and its family tree, including firm favourites such as the Mimosa and Brandy Alexander, and cocktails that will challenge your tastebuds like the Sazerac or the Corpse Reviver.

# Kir Royale

**Ingredients**
- 100ml of Champagne
- 2 tsp of Blackcurrant Liqueur
- Raspberries, for garnish

**You Will Need**
- 50ml Measure

**Method**

Add the Blackcurrant Liqueur to a glass

Top up with Champagne

Garnish with Raspberries

**Ingredients**
- 50ml of Peach Puree
- 100ml of Champagne
- Peach Slice, for Garnish

**You Will Need**
- 50ml Measure
- Bar Spoon

For more information on bar tools, see page 8

# Bellini

## Mimosa | Rossini

**Method**

Add the Peach Puree to a glass

Then add the Champagne

Stir gently to combine

Garnish with a Peach Slice

- For a Mimosa, swap the Peach Puree for Orange Juice and garnish with a Cherry or a Strawberry
- For a Rossini, swap the Peach Puree for Strawberry Puree and garnish with a Strawberry

## Ingredients

- 50ml of Brandy
- 3 tsp of Sweet Vermouth
- 3 tsp of Simple Syrup
- 1 Dash of Angostura Bitters
- Ice Cubes
- Orange Peel, for garnish

## You Will Need

- 50ml Measure
- Cocktail Shaker
- Strainer

For more information on bar tools, see page 8

# Harvard

## Method

Add all of the ingredients to a Cocktail Shaker filled with ice

Shake until the cocktail shaker is cold to the touch

Strain into a glass

Garnish with Orange Peel

**Ingredients**
**To make approximately 2 litres**
- 900ml of Brandy
- 450ml of Jamaican Rum
- 225ml of Lemon Juice
- 225ml of Curaçao
- 225ml of Simple Syrup
- Crushed Ice

**You Will Need**
- 25ml Measure
- 50ml Measure
- Bar Spoon

# Curaçao Punch

## Method

Add all the ingredients to a Punch Bowl or Cocktail Fish Bowl

Top up with Crushed Ice

Stir to combine

Garnish with exotic fruits of your choice

## Ingredients
- 50ml of Cognac or Brandy
- 25ml of Orange Liqueur
- 25ml of Lemon Juice
- Ice Cubes

## You Will Need
- 25ml Measure
- 50ml Measure
- Cocktail Shaker
- Strainer
- Reamer

For more information on bar tools, see page 8

# Sidecar

**Method**

Add all of the ingredients to a Cocktail Shaker filled with ice

Shake until the cocktail shaker is cold to the touch

Strain into a glass

# Corpse Reviver No.1

## Ingredients
- 50ml of Cognac
- 25ml of Apple Brandy
- 25ml of Sweet Vermouth
- Ice Cubes

## You Will Need
- 25ml Measure
- 50ml Measure
- Mixing Glass
- Bar Spoon

## Method

Add the ingredients to a Mixing Glass filled with ice

Stir well to combine

Pour into a glass

# Black Velvet

**Ingredients**
- 100ml of Stout
- Champagne

**You Will Need**
- 50ml Measure

**Method**

Half fill a glass with
Champagne

Top up with Stout

# Nantucket

## Ingredients
- 50ml of Brandy
- 25ml of Cranberry Juice
- 25ml of Grapefruit Juice
- Ice Cubes
- Lime Slice, for garnish

## You Will Need
- 25ml Measure
- 50ml Measure
- Mixing Glass
- Strainer
- Bar Spoon

## Method

Add the ingredients to a Mixing Glass filled with ice

Stir gently to combine

Strain into a glass

Garnish with a Lime Slice

# Brandy Sour

## Ingredients
- 50ml of Brandy
- 25ml of Lemon Juice
- 3 tsp of Simple Syrup
- 3 Dashes of Angostura Bitters
- ½ an Egg White
- Ice Cubes
- Lemon Slice and Cherries for garnish

## You Will Need
- 25ml Measure
- 50ml Measure
- Cocktail Shaker

## Method

Add all of the ingredients to a Cocktail Shaker filled with ice

Shake until the cocktail shaker is cold to the touch

Pour into a glass

Garnish with a Lemon Slice and Cherries

# Brandy Alexander

## Ingredients
- 25ml of Cognac
- 25ml of Chocolate Liqueur
- 25ml of Fresh Cream
- Grated Nutmeg, for garnish

## You Will Need
- 25ml Measure
- Cocktail Shaker
- Strainer

## Method

Add all of the ingredients to a Cocktail Shaker filled with Ice

Shake until the cocktail shaker is cold to the touch

Strain into a glass

Garnish with Grated Nutmeg

# Sazerac

**Ingredients**
- 75ml of Brandy
- 75ml of Chilled Water
- 2 Dashes of Peychaud's Bitters
- 3 tsp of Absinthe
- 2 tsp of Simple Syrup
- Ice Cubes
- Lemon Peel, for garnish

**You Will Need**
- 25ml Measure
- Mixing Glass
- Bar Spoon
- Strainer

**Method**

Pour the Chilled Water into a glass, add the Absinthe and set aside

Add the Brandy, Bitters and Simple Syrup to a Mixing Glass, top up with Ice Cubes and stir gently to combine

Discard the Water and Absinthe mixture, strain the cocktail from the Mixing Glass into the chilled glass and garnish with Lemon Peel

# Index

# Acknowledgement

drinkstuff.com would like to thank the following contributors, without whom this book would not have been possible.

Photography: Sally Burt, Laura Stagg
Editor: James Seber